500 GREETINGS

Invitations, Greeting cards,
Postcards & Self-promotion
material

In memoriam: Conxi Papió

500 Greetings
Invitations, Greeting cards,
Postcards & Self-promotion
material

Selection of contents:
Marta Serrats/David Lorente/
Claudia Parra
Foreword © David Lorente
English translation:
Sarah Frutos Bambery/Tom Corkett
Layout & cover design:
spread: David Lorente with Claudia Parra,
and Conxi Papió

Back cover
© Frenzy, Violaine & Jérémy
© X'mas for friends, Tseng Kuo-Chan
© Face Stamp!, Human After All
© Connecting the Dots, Ji-Young Jeon
© Material Art Fair, Anagrama

Inner cover
© Philographics, Studio Carreras
© The Joy of Graphic Design, I Like Birds
© The Diary of Anne Frank, Maira Purman
© Blaustein / Melting, Melina Pecharki
© Keet & Luuk, Me Studio
© Latin American Design Festival 2015,
 Is Creative Studio

Promopress is a brand of:
Promotora de Prensa Internacional S.A.
C/ Ausiàs Marc 124
08013 Barcelona, Spain
Phone: +34 93 245 14 64
Fax: +34 93 265 48 83
email: info@promopress.es
www.promopresseditions.com
Facebook: Promopress Editions
Twitter: Promopress Editions @PromopressEd

Printed in China.

500

GREETINGS

Invitations, Greeting cards, Postcards,
& Self-promotion material

INTRODUCTION

Communi-action Projects

David Lorente

Among the pages of this book, you will find a selection of graphic proposals that share a common denominator: they aim to create a personal situation where the transmitter is brought closer to the receiver. We could label them *proximity projects*: in the same way that we increasingly seek out local products in the market that bring us closer to the farmer that cultivated them, some messages successfully reduce the distance between those who produce and those who receive them.

There are various ways in which these projects reach their goal, and I cite only a few: the scale of the proposal's intervention—small, the receiver can reach it straight away; an intimate, warm and friendly tone that avoids formalities; the construction of simple messages with no small print; choice, far removed from the standards and from certain support materials which seek to make the haptic experience more sophisticated for the person who receives the object, with the aim of giving it a certain intimacy. Here, the designer seeks to get closer to people and does so in such a way that the graphic proposal shows the most genuine, most real—in other words more personal—face of the person speaking to us.

When I saw these proposals, one the most salient aspects seemed to be their ability to inspire action. I am referring to the fact that, in order to respond fully to the received communication, it is necessary to involve the user so that they activate the specific mechanisms proposed by the piece. This means that the piece acts as a mechanism with a suggestive potential for activity. We find that it is no longer enough to wait for the receiver to interpret a graphic piece, they need to feel impelled to act. And so, as graphic designers, we must begin to think beyond composing, reticulating, selecting typefaces, colour, etc. We have to incorporate new verbs into our professional dictionary: to accumulate, to combine, to compile, to customise, to facet, to generate layers, to geometrise, to integrate, to interfere, to multiply, *to objectify,* to package, to stitch...

At the same time the user-receiver ceases to be passive and also assumes new tasks: activating, assembling/disassembling, colourising, cropping, daubing, die-cutting, discovering/hiding, folding/unfolding, joining/separating, manipulating, opening/closing, piercing, pressing, processing, rearranging, reproducing, ripping, stamping, sticking/unsticking, stretching, superimposing, twisting, tying/untying...

In some of the proposals that we have selected for this book we can see how these objects operate—it is no longer merely a question of graphics! They are devices that stimulate proactive communication; could we call it *communi-action*?

When we announce some of the projects from the selection, we invite you to enjoy a rich and diverse landscape that demonstrates graphics-object proximity through illustration, pop-up or printing techniques.

David Lorente is a graphic designer who specialises in the field of publishing and, together with Tomoko Sakamoto, created the Spread team, based in Barcelona. Currently he is teaching at Barcelona's Escola Elisava.

CONTENTS

AUTHORS INDEX

London
and You
MERCEDES LEÓN

CLIENT
Self-promotion

CITY
London, UK

This project was produced
by illustrator and designer
Mercedes León during the
first year of her master's
degree in illustration.
It explores the boundaries
of one's own identity in
an urban environment.
Playing with scales and
sizes, Mercedes manages to
convey a vision of the world
from a child's perspective.

I CAN'T
DRAW THE
BEST THING
OF LONDON:
THE SMELL
OF FRIED
CHICKEN

Eu & Tu

STUDIO AH—HA
for TODAY IS THE DAY

CLIENT
Self-promotion

CITY
Lisbon, PT

Eu & Tu (You and Me) is a conceptual project that is characterized by its very intimate air and its use of simple lines and black ink. It was designed by Today is the Day for a wedding.

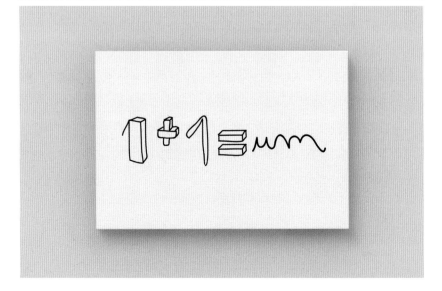

London Family Portrait

MERCEDES LEÓN

CLIENT
Personal work

CITY
London, UK

This series of nine postcards that present popular faces from the social and political scene in Britain was created by illustrator and designer Mercedes León for a group exhibition in the Loom Room of Blackall Studios in London.

Boris Johnson
London Major

Margaret Thatcher
The Iron Lady

Charles Dickens
Writer & novelist

Mary Portas
Queen of Shops

3

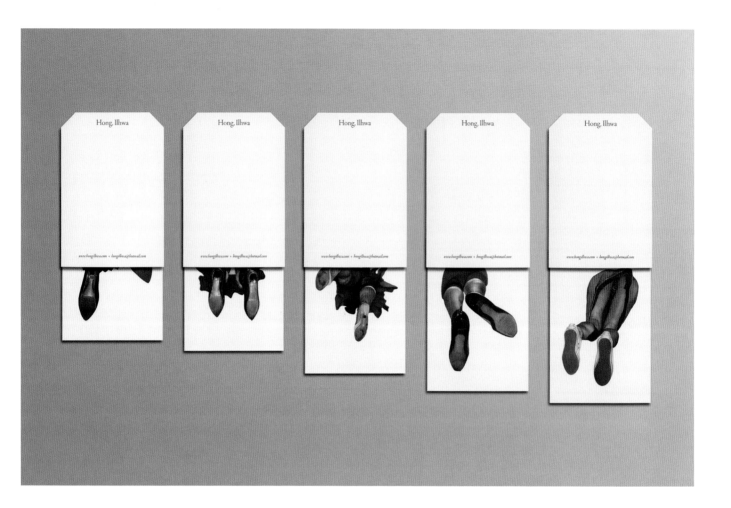

Hong Ilhwa
Business Cards
HUNDREDS

CLIENT
Hong Ilhwa

CITY
Seoul, KR

The Seoul-based visual and editorial agency Hundreds was hired to design business cards for the Korean artist Ilhwa Hong. The cards that they created are based on Hong's series of paintings centred on women's bodies. The very simple envelopes have cut-out corners so that the card inside completes the quadrangular form.

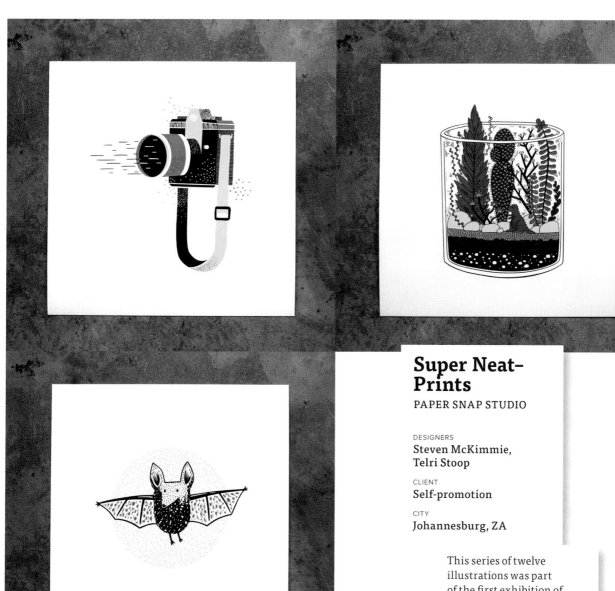

Super Neat–Prints

PAPER SNAP STUDIO

DESIGNERS
**Steven McKimmie,
Telri Stoop**

CLIENT
Self-promotion

CITY
Johannesburg, ZA

This series of twelve illustrations was part of the first exhibition of prints made by Paper Snap in Johannesburg. Limited editions were presented during the Super Neat exhibition, where a live screen-printing performance promoted the workshops offered by the designers.

Postcards from Clerkenwell

MERCEDES LEÓN

CLIENT
**Creative Clerkenwell
and Craft Central**

CITY
London, UK

This design by illustrator Mercedes León was created in collaboration with Creative Clerkenwell for the Clerkenwell Design Week 2013, during which architectural walking tours were organized to show the rich heritage and history of London's Clerkenwell district.

ST JAMES'S CHURCH

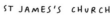

MARX MEMORIAL

OLD SESSIONS HOUSE

CLERKENWELL GREEN

CRAF

JERUSALEM
TAVERN

MOUNTFORD HOUSE

COWCROSS ST

GOLDSMITHS' CENTRE & CAFE

ST PETER'S
LANE

PASSING
ALLEYS

TURNMILL

FARRINGDON

ON WORKS

TUBE & RAIL STATION

RDS FROM CLERKENWELL

THE CROWN

EXMOUTH MARKET

ST PAUL'S

BARBICAN

WATCHMAKERS

BOWLING GREEN LANE

FINSBURY TOWN HALL

FT CENTRAL

RAL SHOP & STUDIOS

CRAFT CENTRAL

CRAFT CENTRAL GALLERY & STUDIOS

ST JOHN'S SQUARE

PRINTWORKS

CLERKENWELL ROAD

N'S GATE

N'S ST

FARMILOE & SONS

FARMILOE MERCHANTS

LANSONS' COURTYARD

CHARTERHOUSE SQUARE

SMITHFIELD MKT

SMITHFIELD CENTRAL MARKET

ST BARTHOLOMEW CHURCH

Anne Cecile

STUDIO AH—HA
for TODAY IS THE DAY

ILLUSTRATOR
Mariana Salmeiro

CITY
Lisbon, PT

This invitation was designed
by Today is the Day / Studio
AH-HA for a private
birthday party. The project
consists of black cards
with different elements
combined in a collage.
The invitations come in
black envelopes that evoke
the nocturnal character
of the event.

X'mas
for friends
TSENG KUO-CHAN

CLIENT
Self-promotion

CITY
Taipei, TW

Taiwanese designer Tseng Kuo-Chan created this card to wish friends and clients a Merry Christmas.
The font, the logo and the composition were designed specifically for the project.

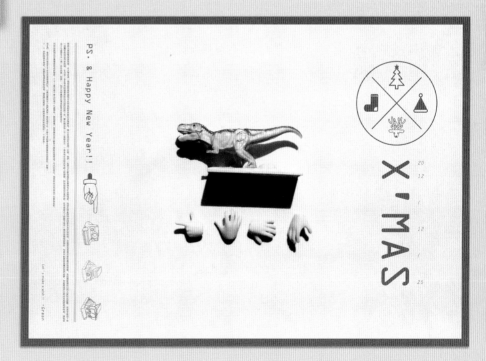

Joana & Tiago

STUDIO AH—HA
for TODAY IS THE DAY

ILLUSTRADOR
Francisca Magalhães

CITY
Lisbon, PT

The lavish design of these wedding invitations includes fruits, flamingos, palm trees and maps—a wide variety of natural and geographical elements that reveal the personalities of the couple to be married.

outro dia em arraiolos

cabo verde

em direção ao algarve

em sevilha

e albufeira

na praia

dos salgados

em

reguengos de monsaraz

de piodão

coimbra

foi uma canção

Frenzy

VIOLAINE & JÉRÉMY

ILLUSTRATION
Jérémy Schneider

CLIENT
Frenzy Paris

CITY
Paris, FR

These branding and promotional materials for the Paris-based audiovisual producer Frenzy feature a completely personalized font that was created especially for the firm, as well as illustrations for its various communication platforms and events.

Rooted in Love Wedding

APARTMENT ONE

CREATIVE DIRECTORS
**Liza Lowinger,
Simon Isaacs,
Spencer Bagley**

DESIGNERS
**Spencer Bagley,
Janet Kim**

ILLUSTRATOR
Bonnie Clas

CLIENT
**Liza Lowinger,
Simon Isaacs**

CITY
New York, USA

The wedding invitations and supplementary materials in this project include illustrated elements of the couple's homes of Brooklyn and Vermont. Guests were given a cookbook containing friends' and relatives' favourite recipes.

Liza & Simon

WEDDING WEEKEND
June 22-24, 2012

Friday

welcome party
bentleys restaurant
9:00 pm

Saturday

local activities

Saturday

wedding ceremony & reception
the barnard inn
5:00 pm

Sunday

farewell brunch
the blue horse inn
9:30 am – 1:00 pm

for more weekend details
and travel information

visit lizaandsimon.com

---

their families

LA LOWINGER
— & —
COLO FRANCESCO ISAACS

invite you to share in the joy
of their wedding day

Saturday, June 23, 2012
five o'clock

The Barnard Inn
old route twelve
barnard, vermont
—

feast and merriment to follow the ceremony
summer formal attire

---

please join us for our

TRADITIONAL KOREAN CEREMONY
— and —
FAMILY REHEARSAL DINNER

Friday, June 22, 2012
five o'clock

Cloudland Farm
1101 cloudland road
north pomfret, vermont
—

please rsvp to hello@lizaandsimon.com
or make a note on your rsvp card

—
COMMUNITY COOKBOOK
—

we're collecting a favorite recipe
from our friends and family and combining them
into a community cookbook to share with you

please submit your recipe at
lizaandsimon.com

2nd of june

Postcards
from Morocco
BIANCA TSCHAIKNER

CLIENT
Self-promotion

CITY
Porto, PT

Bianca Tschaikner's personal experiences
Morocco provided the inspiration for this
series of twelve postcards that depict anecdotes
and observations of locals' everyday lives.
The content of the illustrations moves away
from the romantic cliché of the *Arabian Nights*.

The Diary
of Anne Frank Postcards

MAIRA PURMAN

CLIENT
Petiteposte

CITY
Barcelona, SP

The story of Anne Frank is the inspiration behind these postcards designed by Maira Purman. Nearly seventy years after its publication, her diary is as powerful as ever. Anne's wish was accomplished: "I want to go on living even after my death."

13

BCMG Family Concert/
Curiouser & Curiouser
MINA BRAUN

CLIENT
**Birmingham
Contemporary Music Group**

CITY
Birmingham, UK

Mina Braun's artwork is strongly influenced by narratives: by connecting people and nature she creates a powerful symbolism for the emotions of her characters. This is a selection of works commissioned by the Birmingham Contemporary Music Group to announce their upcoming events, and by the Scottish Gallery Curiouser & Curiouser. These works show Mina's vision and her unique representation of dreamlike atmospheres.

Ich liebe Dich wie Apfelmuß 2013

I LIKE BIRDS

CLIENT
BB-Schoenfelderhof

CITY
Hamburg, DE

I Like Birds designed this invitation card and poster presentation for a poetry and illustration exhibition organized to publicize the works of different artists from psychiatric institutions. The agency also designed the book that contains the artists' works.

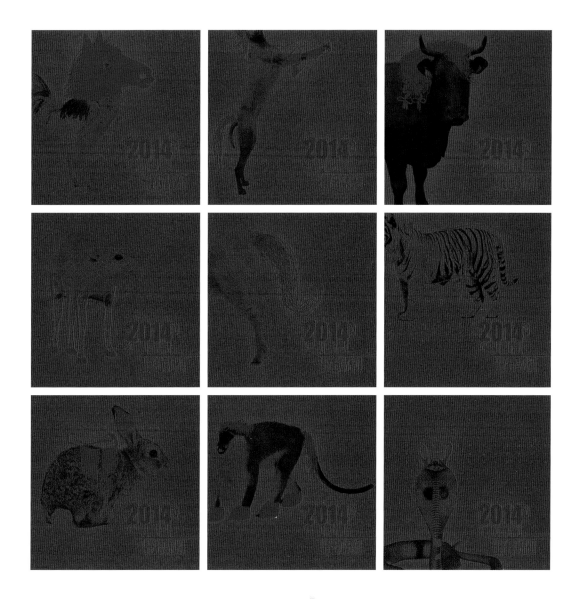

2014 Dragon
OLGA NOVYKOVA

CLIENT
Personal work

CITY
Kherson, UA

This series of Christmas cards was design by Olga Novykova. According to the Chinese zodiac, 2014 was the year of the horse. To celebrate it, the designer presents different animals that have been embellished with equine features, through which the other animals pay homage to the creature of that year.

Quintas do Conservatório – Sagração da Primavera

ORAVIVA! DESIGNERS

DESIGNERS
Nuno Campos, Luísa Beato

CLIENT
A2C2

CITY
Coimbra, Santa Maria de Feira, PT

Quintas do Conservatório is a cultural event that takes place at the *Coimbra Music Conservatory* twice a year, in the spring and autumn. Oraviva! designers' graphics for the spring were inspired by the flowered gardens of that season. Illustrations of plants in bloom decorate the event's posters, flyers and invitations.

Today is the Day
STUDIO AH—HA

DESIGNER
Mariana Sameiro

CLIENT
Self-promotion

CITY
Lisbon, PT

Studio AH-HA created this promotional
stationery and accompanying logos as part
of its Today is the Day project, which focuses
on producing materials for special events
such as parties, birthdays and weddings.

Adam + Dorian
DANIEL IOANNOU

CLIENT
**Adam Kuperman
+ Dorian Ferlauto**

CITY
Sydney, AU

Adam Kuperman and Dorian Ferlauto
commissioned the designer Daniel Ioannou
to produce stationery and invitations for
a special weekend event for their friends
and family. The invitations were inspired
by the place chosen for the celebration,
Chileno Valley Ranch in California.
They feature a palette of greens and vintage
botanical illustrations. The invitations were
delivered in luxury cream-coloured envelopes.

Medamothi Planum
STEFANIE BRÜCKLER

CLIENT
Harald Stojan

CITY
Graz, AT

This project is part of composer Belma Beslic-Gal's piece Medamothi Planum, which narrates a journey through outer space. Sound artist Harald Stojan commissioned the design for the CD packaging as well as for the poster and flyer for the presentation of the project at the SAE Institute in Vienna. The design was inspired by the surface of Triton, one of Neptune's moons.

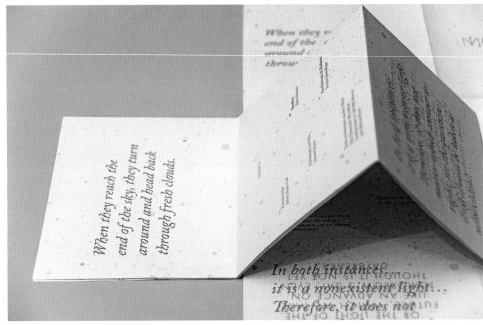

VRtoSA

STUDIO AH—HA

CLIENT
Saraiva e Associados

CITY
Lisbon, PT

The historical centre of Vila Real de Santo António in southern Portugal is the focus of this project. All the graphic elements were designed based on four elements that represent the city: the water of the sea, river and estuary; the orthogonal street grid; Manuel Cabanas's wood-engraved illustrations; and António Aleixo's poems.

21

high wheel safety bike

kids bike

tandem bike

penny-farthing bike

randonneur bike

ladies bike

commuter bike

flat bar road bike

Maria & Pedro

STUDIO AH—HA
for TODAY IS THE DAY

CITY
Lisbon, PT

Portugal's Studio AH-HA designed this wedding invitation as part of its parallel project Today is the Day. The postcard-format invitation came with a choice of white envelopes that feature illustrations of human-powered vehicles, including bicycles, tandems and tricycles.

Warm Wishes From the Netherlands

WENG NAM YAP

CLIENT
**Weng Nam Yap,
Haruka Yamada**

CITY
Kuala Lumpur, MY

Weng Nam Yap designed
this Christmas card for
friends and family on
the other side of the globe.
The alphabet incorporates
traditional Dutch elements
and experimentation with
engraving and silk-screen
techniques.

Pernod Ricard Portugal Christmas Card

STUDIO AH—HA for TODAY IS THE DAY & CO

CLIENT
Pernod Ricard Portugal

CITY
Lisbon, PT

Portugal's landscapes were the inspiration for this timeless, simple and elegant Christmas card designed for this legendary distillery.

Rice Invite
RICE CREATIVE

CLIENT
Rice Creative

CITY
Ho Chi Minh City, VN

For the opening of Rice Creative's new offices, the team designed a cryptic invitation containing a message to decipher. Once the invitation is opened, it turns into a paper rice bowl with recognizable Asian influences.

SÃO PEDRO

(e todos os outros)

lá em casa!

28 Junho 2014

20.30

São Pedro

STUDIO AH—HA
for TODAY IS THE DAY

ILLUSTRATOR
**Francisca Magalhães
Ramalho**

CITY
Lisbon, PT

This invitation for the São
Pedro Festival is the work
of Portugal's Studio AH-HA.
This naïve yet sophisticated
work is part of the agency's
Today is the Day project.

Letterpressed Geek Gods Calendar 2013

PUBLICIS MACHINE

EXECUTIVE CREATIVE DIRECTORS
**Jake Bester,
Gareth McPherson**

DESIGN DIRECTOR
Dani Loureiro

ILLUSTRATORS & DESIGNERS
**Dani Loureiro,
Andrew Ringrose**

CLIENT
Habari Media

CITY
Cape Town, ZA

Every year, Habari Media creates a bespoke calendar highlighting twelve media industry leaders. This year, the chosen concept was "Geek Gods", playing up their prowess and intelligence. The metaphor of Geek God and Geek Goddess extended into the execution, graphics and writing. Details of each personality were interpreted and translated into representing each individual as a new 'Geek God or Goddess'. The calendar includes an accurate lunar calendar and is constructed with reference to a sun dial, intended to be used as a marker for each date which can be moved around manually.

Miel & Tuur
JACQUES & LISE

CLIENT
Birth announcement card

CITY
Diest, BE

Designers and partners Jacques & Lise
created this unique folded card to announce
the birth of twins.

Keet & Luuk
ME STUDIO

CLIENT
Personal work
CITY
Amsterdam, NL

These three-dimensional cards were designed to announce the births of the designer's two children. The design was printed in two Pantone colours, and the pop-up letters and fold lines were die cut with a special laser and hand folded.

Azede
Jean-Pierre
SS15 Invite
JOSEPH VEAZEY

CLIENT
Self-promotion

CITY
London, UK

The presentation of the spring/summer 2015 collection by designer Azede Jean-Pierre took its inspiration from gardens and nature. On one side, the invitation to the show features a hand-painted font made up of plant pots, which is used to spell out "SS15." On the reverse, an illustration of a garden with three labels reveals the details of the show.

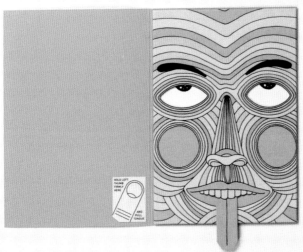

Personal Holiday Card

JOSEPH VEAZEY

CLIENT
Self-promotion

CITY
New York, USA

This greeting card for the festive season was created by Joseph Veazey. Pulling the tongue brings the face to life by causing the eyes to close and display the card's holiday greetings message.

31

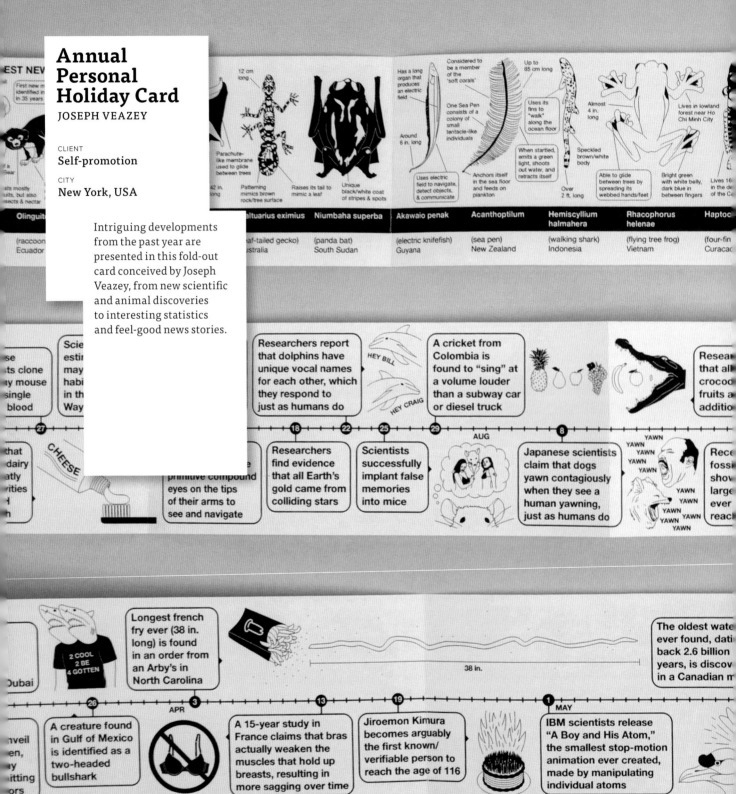

Annual Personal Holiday Card

JOSEPH VEAZEY

CLIENT
Self-promotion

CITY
New York, USA

Intriguing developments from the past year are presented in this fold-out card conceived by Joseph Veazey, from new scientific and animal discoveries to interesting statistics and feel-good news stories.

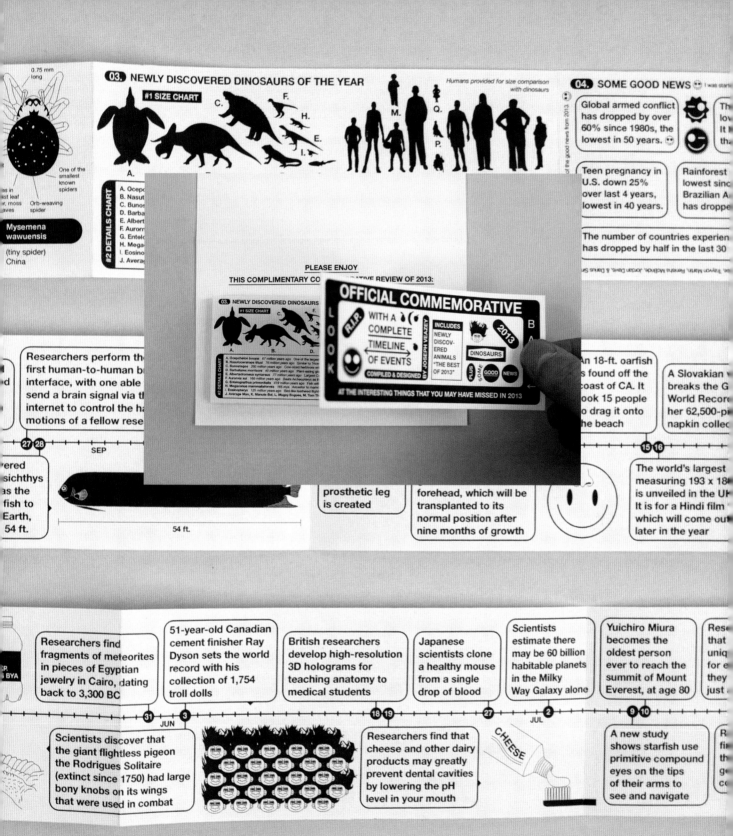

03. NEWLY DISCOVERED DINOSAURS OF THE YEAR

#1 SIZE CHART

Humans provided for size comparison with dinosaurs

C. F. H. E. I. A. M. Q. P.

#2 DETAILS CHART

A. Ocepo
B. Nasut
C. Bunos
D. Barba
E. Albert
F. Aurorn
G. Entelo
H. Mega
I. Eosino
J. Averag

0.75 mm long

as in
Nasut leaf
er, moss
aves

One of the smallest known spiders

Orb-weaving spider

Mysemena wawuensis

(tiny spider)
China

04. SOME GOOD NEWS ☺ I was startl

Global armed conflict has dropped by over 60% since 1980s, the lowest in 50 years. ☺

Teen pregnancy in U.S. down 25% over last 4 years, lowest in 40 years.

Rainforest lowest sinc Brazilian A has droppe

The number of countries experien has dropped by half in the last 30

PLEASE ENJOY
THIS COMPLIMENTARY CO....RATIVE REVIEW OF 2013:

OFFICIAL COMMEMORATIVE

LOOK

R.I.P.

WITH A COMPLETE TIMELINE OF EVENTS

COMPILED & DESIGNED

INCLUDES NEWLY DISCOV- ERED ANIMALS "THE BEST OF 2013"

2013

DINOSAURS

PLUS SOME GOOD NEWS

B A

03. NEWLY DISCOVERED DINOSAURS
#1 SIZE CHART

AT THE INTERESTING THINGS THAT YOU MAY HAVE MISSED IN 2013

Researchers perform the first human-to-human b.... interface, with one able ... send a brain signal via th.... internet to control the ha.... motions of a fellow rese....

27 28 SEP

....ered ...sichthys ...as the ...fish to ...Earth, ...54 ft.

54 ft.

An 18-ft. oarfish ..s found off the coast of CA. It ..ook 15 people .o drag it onto .he beach

A Slovakian breaks the G World Recor her 62,500-p napkin collec

15 16

The world's largest measuring 193 x 18.. is unveiled in the UK It is for a Hindi film which will come ou later in the year

prosthetic leg is created

forehead, which will be transplanted to its normal position after nine months of growth

---

Researchers find fragments of meteorites in pieces of Egyptian jewelry in Cairo, dating back to 3,300 BC

51-year-old Canadian cement finisher Ray Dyson sets the world record with his collection of 1,754 troll dolls

British researchers develop high-resolution 3D holograms for teaching anatomy to medical students

Japanese scientists clone a healthy mouse from a single drop of blood

Scientists estimate there may be 60 billion habitable planets in the Milky Way Galaxy alone

Yuichiro Miura becomes the oldest person ever to reach the summit of Mount Everest, at age 80

Rese that uniq for e they just

31 JUN **3** **18 19** **27** JUL **2** **9 10**

Scientists discover that the giant flightless pigeon the Rodrigues Solitaire (extinct since 1750) had large bony knobs on its wings that were used in combat

Researchers find that cheese and other dairy products may greatly prevent dental cavities by lowering the pH level in your mouth

CHEESE

A new study shows starfish use primitive compound eyes on the tips of their arms to see and navigate

R fi th g ju

Super Neat Zine #2

PAPER SNAP STUDIO

DESIGNERS
**Steven McKimmie,
Telri Stoop**

CLIENT
Self-promotion

CITY
Johannesburg, ZA

The curious characters that feature in this self-published fold-out illustrated by Paper Snap present us with their favourite dishes. The work is part of a mini-collection of brochures and can be displayed on a wall.

Snap To It!
PAPER SNAP STUDIO

DESIGNERS
**Steven McKimmie,
Telri Stoop**

CLIENT
Self-promotion

CITY
Johannesburg, ZA

This promotional card is folded and bound as if it were a small gift. It was designed to attract potential customers and promote Paper Snap's new website.

34

Petit Maison-Tags
PAPER SNAP STUDIO

DESIGNERS
**Steven McKimmie,
Telri Stoop**

CLIENT
Self-promotion

CITY
Johannesburg, ZA

Paper Snap came up with the idea for these gift tags during a trip to Belgium. The tags are inspired by the simple geometric shapes of the country's houses.

Michele Forzano
Lorenzo Perucconi

Central studio
Design—Communication
Lugano

Buone feste
e felice anno nuovo

ALBERO
DA ALBERO

www.centralstudio.ch

2015

Albero da Albero
CENTRAL STUDIO

CLIENT
Self-promotion

CITY
Lugano, CH

Lugano-based Central Studio produced this Christmas card for its customers, members and friends. Inspired by Little Trees, the most popular car air freshener in the world, this little pine tree makes a perfect Christmas tree ornament. Each year, Central Studio creates a new background, but the design always remains the same.

36

Food Fight
TRAPPED IN SUBURBIA

DESIGNERS
**Karin Langeveld,
Cuby Gerards,
Richard Fussey**

CLIENT
Trapped in Suburbia

CITY
The Hague, NL

The ingenious Food Fight notepad designed by Trapped in Suburbia is a follow-up to the team's Play More pad. Write a message, tear off the sheet, make it into a ball, and you're ready to start a food fight! The designs featured include spaghetti, cake and chips.

The End Age

RICE CREATIVE

CLIENT
Rice Creative

CITY
Ho Chi Minh City, VN

This collaboration between Rice Creative and photographer Arnaud De Harven yielded these unusual invitations for an exhibition of the artist's work. They feature a strip of 35 mm film that reveals the details of the event when the tab is pulled.

Teepee

DEVICE

DESIGNERS
**Ross Clodfelter,
Shane Cranford**

CLIENT
Lisa Vorce

CITY
Winston-Salem, NC, USA

To announce a marriage ceremony that would take place in the Arizona desert, wedding organizer Lisa Vorce devised an invitation that honours Native American culture. Device Creative was responsible for designing the invitation in the form of a tepee held up by bamboo poles.

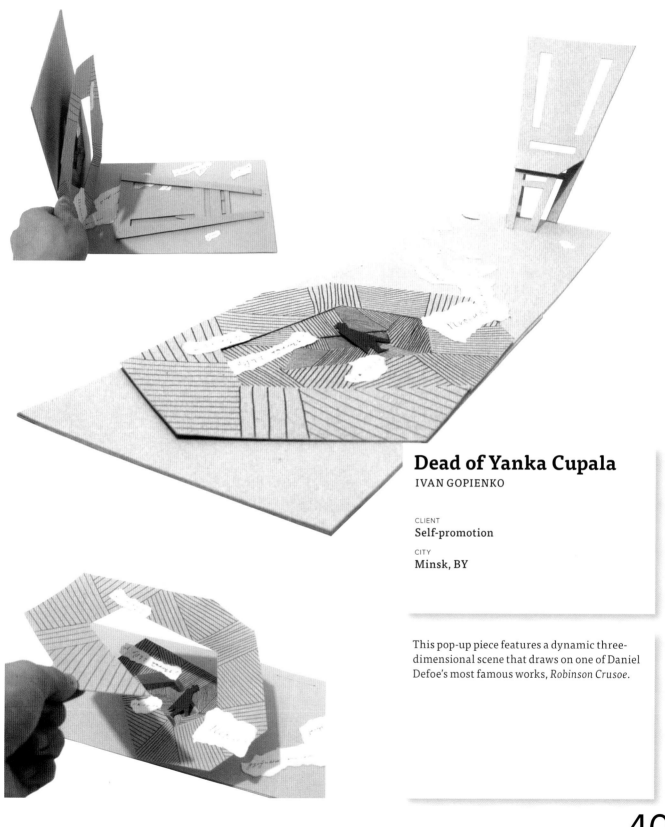

Dead of Yanka Cupala

IVAN GOPIENKO

CLIENT
Self-promotion

CITY
Minsk, BY

This pop-up piece features a dynamic three-dimensional scene that draws on one of Daniel Defoe's most famous works, *Robinson Crusoe*.

Valentine's Vouchers

VERONIKA PLANT

CLIENT
Personal work

CITY
Fürth, DE

Each of the twenty-four handmade "love coupons" in this collection contains a unique and personal detail. It was created as a Valentine's Day gift and is presented in a painted box.

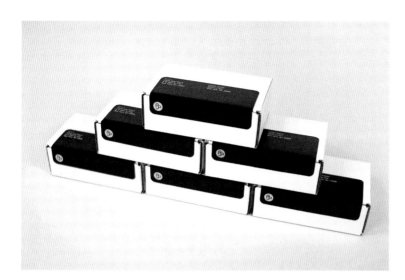

Azede Jean-Pierre
SS14 Invite

JOSEPH VEAZEY

CLIENT
Azede Jean-Pierre

CITY
New York, NY, USA

This invitation was designed for the presentation of designer Azede Jean-Pierre's spring/summer 2014 collection, which consisted of prints and shapes inspired by beetles, sea slugs and other small animals. Invitees received a small cube of transparent plastic resin containing an insect as a gift.

OLGA NOVYKOVA

CLIENT
Personal work

CITY
Kherson, UA

Designer Olga Novykova's Christmas postcards provide fun and practical tips for getting through the winter season and keeping warm. Who would argue with a grandmother's advice to change out of wet socks?

ЩО ЗІГРІВАЄ НАЙЛІПШЕ

КОЛИ ХОЛОДНО ВЖИВАЙ ГАРЯЧИЙ ШОКОЛАД АБО ІМБИРНИЙ ЧАЙ

ДОВЕДЕНО АЛЬПІНІСТАМИ

Mubi

ATIPO

CREATIVE DIRECTORS
Raúl García del Pomar, Ismael González

CLIENT
Mubi

CITY
Gijón, SP

To promote its online film service, English firm Mubi sent out these postcards featuring images from classic and contemporary cinema to movie lovers.

As Viagens
de Igor Matka
ORAVIVA! DESIGNERS

DESIGNERS
**Nuno Campos,
Luísa Beato**

CLIENT
All About Dance Academy

CITY
**Coimbra, Santa Maria
de Feira, PT**

Igor Matka's *Journey* tells the story of Igor, a man who imagines a set of characters—one that he too forms a part of—from all over the world. In designing the promotional material for *Journey*, Oraviva! stayed true to the spirit of the original story's multifaceted characters.

Who is the fool?

TRAPPED IN SUBURBIA

DESIGNERS
**Karin Langeveld,
Cuby Gerards**

CLIENT
Dutch Theatre Institute

CITY
The Hague, NL

The exclusive use of black and white for these branding materials for the Hague's Who is the Fool? theatre festival symbolizes the effects of the economic crisis on the culture sector. The festival's logo, stationery, posters, flyers, banners, brochures and website were all produced in this style.

WIE IS DE NAR?

Spelen met   de macht

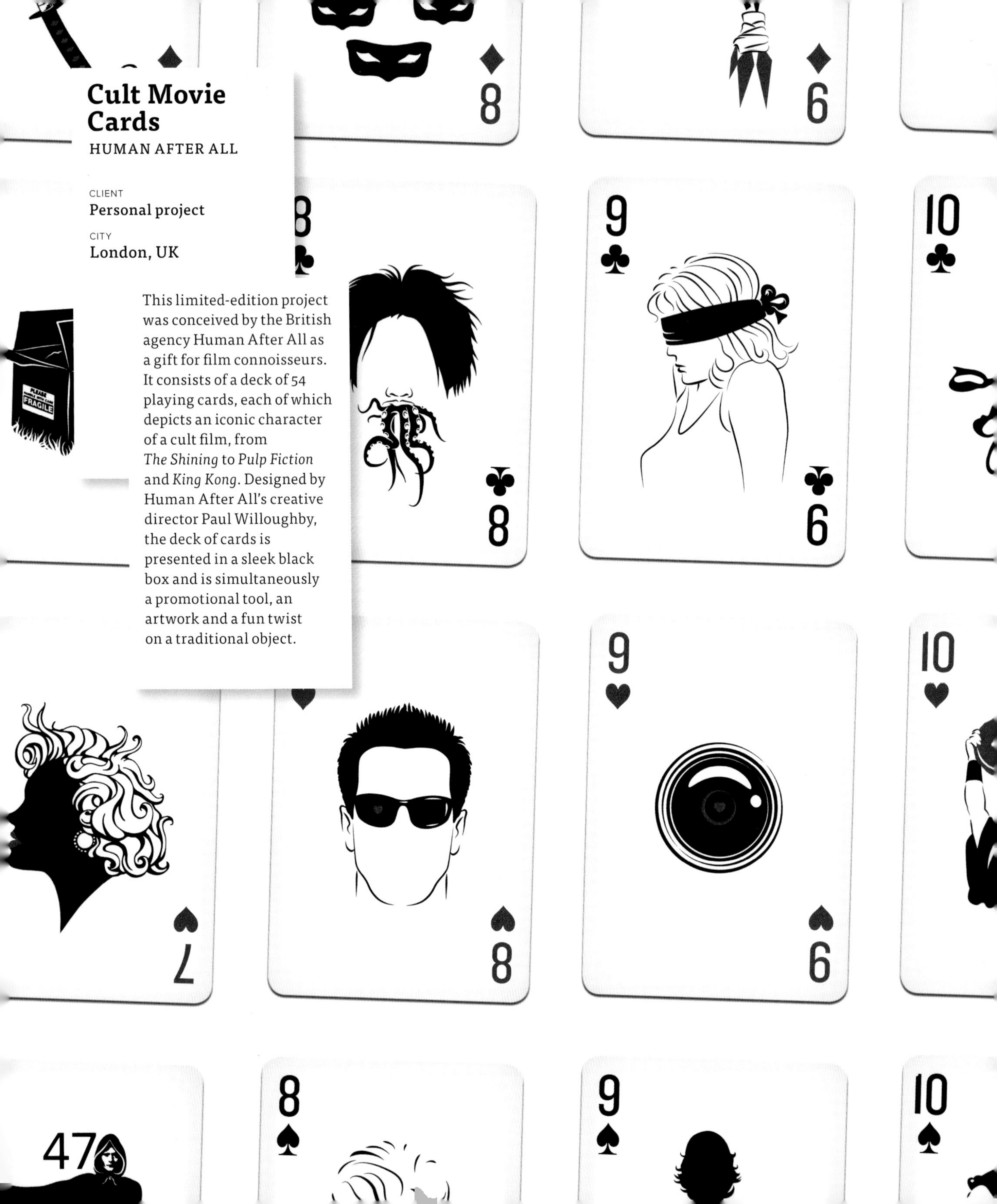

Cult Movie Cards
HUMAN AFTER ALL

CLIENT
Personal project

CITY
London, UK

This limited-edition project was conceived by the British agency Human After All as a gift for film connoisseurs. It consists of a deck of 54 playing cards, each of which depicts an iconic character of a cult film, from *The Shining* to *Pulp Fiction* and *King Kong*. Designed by Human After All's creative director Paul Willoughby, the deck of cards is presented in a sleek black box and is simultaneously a promotional tool, an artwork and a fun twist on a traditional object.

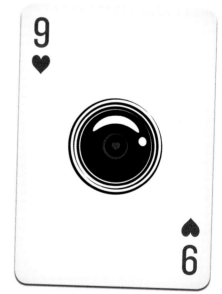

47

Alice
no País das
Maravilhas

ORAVIVA! DESIGNERS

DESIGNERS
**Nuno Campos,
Luísa Beato**

CLIENT
**All About Dance
Academy**

CITY
**Coimbra, Santa Maria
de Feira, PT**

The dance school All About Dance celebrated Christmas with a tribute to Lewis Carroll's Alice in Wonderland. Oraviva designed the poster, flyers, invitations, pins, programs, t-shirts, packaging and even a small stand to sell the t-shirts during the event. The result combines darkness and playfulness in a way that relates very well to the story.

A ALL ABOUT DANCE TEM O PRAZER
DE O(A) CONVIDAR PARA ASSISTIR AO ESPETÁCULO
ALICE NO PAÍS DAS MARAVILHAS NO DIA 21
DE DEZEMBRO ÀS 21:30H NO GRANDE AUDITÓRIO
DO EUROPARQUE EM SANTA MARIA DA FEIRA.

POR FAVOR TROQUE O SEU CONVITE POR UM BILHETE, NA NOITE DO ESPETÁCULO, ATÉ ÀS 21:00H.

49

The Wire Cards

ATIPO

CREATIVE DIRECTOR
**Raúl García del Pomar,
Ismael González**

CLIENT
Personal project

CITY
Gijón, SP

This deck of cards by Atipos Studio pays homage to HBO's hugely popular television series *The Wire*. The portraits on the cards capture the defining features of each of the characters in the series.

Face Stamp!
HUMAN AFTER ALL

CLIENT
Personal project

CITY
London, UK

Face Stamp! is an interactive art experience that allowed visitors to the Pick Me Up 2013 festival to create faces using the features of some of the illustrators. The facial features were presented on ink pads so that visitors could make prints of their creations on cards, paper or t-shirts.

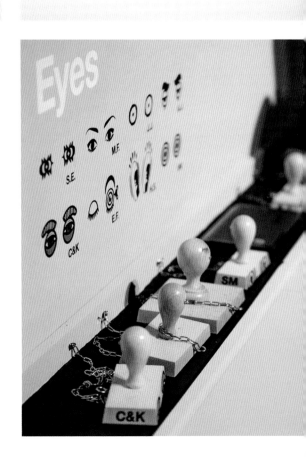

Santa Stamp!
HUMAN AFTER ALL

CLIENT
Personal project

CITY
London, UK

Santa Stamp! was an interactive experience created by Human After All for Selfridges' Destination Christmas Emporium in London. Visitors were able to create their own Christmas cards using ink pads of different festive hats and accessories.

QSL

ALEXANDRA
FOMINSKAYA

CLIENT
Personal project

CTY
Moscow, UR

QSL is a DIY card kit that
includes ink pads with
different letters and
pictograms. Each stamp
has a magnet on the back
that allows you to move it
easily on the steel board.
The kit enables you to create
personalized cards and use
different types of paper,
photographs or newspapers.

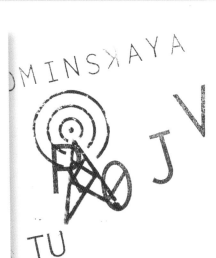

Joana & Ezequiel

MAIRA PURMAN

CLIENT
Joana & Ezequiel

CITY
Rosario, AR

To illustrate this wedding invitation, designer
Maira Purman asked the couple to make a list
of things that were meaningful for them.
She also designed a logo with the name
of the couple, which was used as a seal for
the invitation envelopes.

Stationery line

CARISSIMO
LETTERPRESS

CITY
Vienna, AT

Carissimo Letterpress's stationery line includes elegant wedding stationaries, business cards, one-of a-kind cards for special occasions and letter-writing sets printed on different cotton or recycled papers. Carissimo Letterpress produce and print all their products in Letterpress printing technique with antique printing presses. In Letterpress printing each paper is printed once at a time. For each colour there is a separate print form and print run. Precision, an eye for details and passion for the craft are essential to produce these delicate patterns and colour combinations.

Hey baby!

Merry Christmas

YOU MAKE RIDICULOUSLY EVERY DAY AMAZING

I love Spaghetti (and you)

Merry Christmas & a happy NEW YEAR

ING LINE INE

HAPPY Birthday

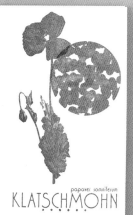

papaver somniferum
KLATSCHMOHN

Life begins after coffee

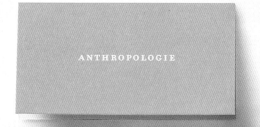

Anthropologie Thanks Card-Spring
MIRIM SEO

ART DIRECTOR
Caroyln Keer,
Jeremy Dean

CLIENT
Anthropologie
Customers

CITY
Philadelphia, PA, USA

The hand stitching and pastel colours in this gift card designed by Mirim Seo for Anthropologie are used to offer the clothing chain's customers both a special message and a tactile experience.

Anthropologie Thanks card

MIRIM SEO

ART DIRECTOR
**Caroyln Keer,
Tram Pham**

CLIENT
**Anthropologie
Customers**

CITY
Philadelphia, PA, USA

Mirim Seo also designed this gift card for Anthropologie. The word "thanks" is hand-stitched on the card.

This is the Beginning of Anything We Want

STEFANIE BRÜCKLER

CLIENT
Personal work

CITY
Graz, AT

The designer, Stefanie Brückler decided to capture the memories, experiences and encounters of a trip in a personal book that compiled a collection of her feelings through typography. The hand-bound book consists of 25 letters - each one a hand-cut memory.

57

I+D Identity
ME STUDIO

CLIENT
I+D

CITY
Amsterdam, NL

A brand identity design
project for a coaching
and training agency run
by two partners with a great
amount of combined
experience. The logo is
created by simple colour
stripes forming a "+" symbol
to underline the importance
of joining knowledge and
savoir faire in a team effort.

58

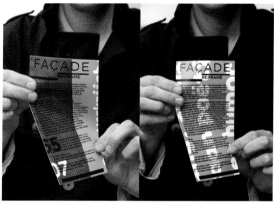

Façade
ME STUDIO

CLIENT
Re: Frame

CITY
Amsterdam, NL

This project consists of a logo and flyers made from recycled advertising-billboard material. It was created for an organization that was launching a design contest aimed at finding uses for the thousands of tons of plastic billboard that are discarded every year. Leaflets of different sizes announcing the contest were printed on reused advertising sheets.

Pokerface
ME STUDIO

CLIENT
Personal work

CITY
Amsterdam, NL

This project was the result of a boring Sunday afternoon in which the designer Martin Pyper realized that he could create a font from a deck of cards. He set about cutting out an alphabet by hand, beginning with the letter "E" and using it to provide the necessary dimensions for the rest of the alphabet deck.

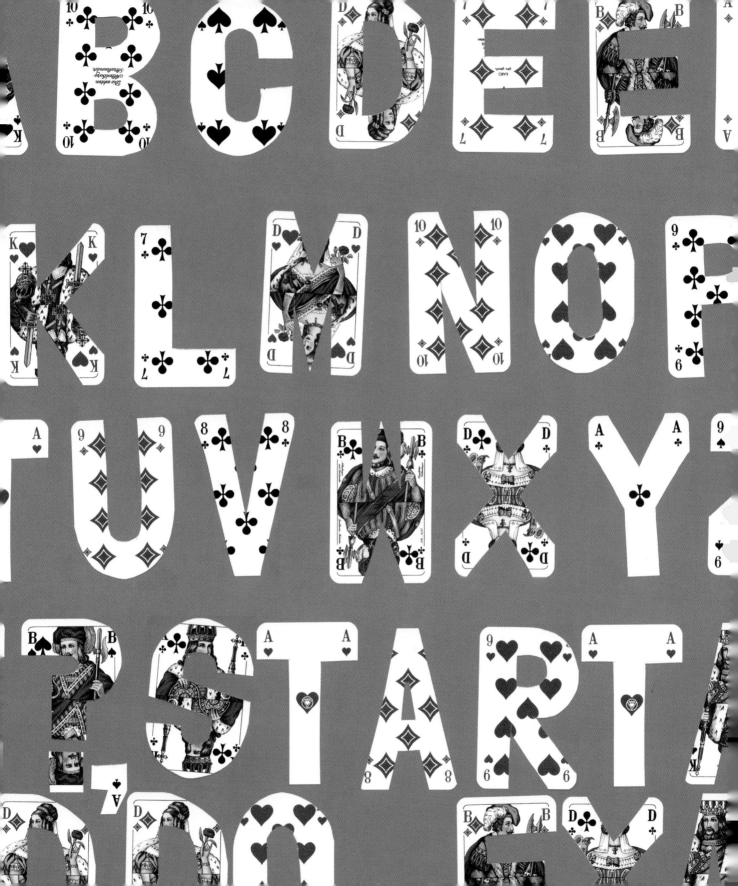

TRIANGLE-STUDIO

Arts&Graphic
Design Partner

www.triangle-studio.co.kr
info@triangle-studio.co.kr

in ma room

TRIANGLE-STUDIO is a arts&
graphic design group for Branding
Editorial Illustration
(all about creative).

We create your brand design
based on rational strategy and
emotional harmony.
Communicate with all things.
Poeple Relationship Communication

Be Triangle!

트라이앵글 스튜디오는 브랜딩, 편집, 일러스트
중심의 아트&그래픽 디자인 회사입니다.

in ma room

TRIANGLE STUDIO

ART DIRECTOR
Kisung Jang

CLIENT
Triangle Studio

CITY
Seoul, KR

in ma room is an
experimental font created
by the Triangle Studio team
and based on the objects
that one might expect to
find in a room. The work was
presented in card and poster
formats.

Krk Folklore Festival
STUDIO 8585

DESIGNERS
**Mario Depicolzuane,
Sabina Barbiš**

CLIENT
Krk Folklore Festival

CITY
**Municipalities
of the island of Krk, HR**

These branding and
promotional materials
were designed for the Krk
Folklore Festival, one of the
oldest folk events in Croatia.
The postcards and posters
feature high-angle shots
of thirteen folk groups
in typical dress.

Oj, Punte, Punte
moj, na moru kitica.
Na moru kitica,
na srcu rožica.

62

Krčki
festival
folklora

Vrbnik, Trg Škujica
9. i 10. srpnja 2011.

Program

Subota 9. srpnja – mlade folklorne skupine

18.30 sati   otvorenje izložbe *Zlatne i srebrne točke*
              autora Sabine Barbiš i Maria Depicolzuane
              zgrada Općine, Trg Škujica
19.30 sati   mimohod mladih folklornih skupina
20.00 sati   početak festivalske priredbe

Nedjelja 10. srpnja – starije folklorne skupine

20.00 sati   mimohod starijih folklornih skupina
20.30 sati   početak festivalske priredbe

Organizator: Općina Vrbnik
Pokrovitelj: Primorsko-goranska županija

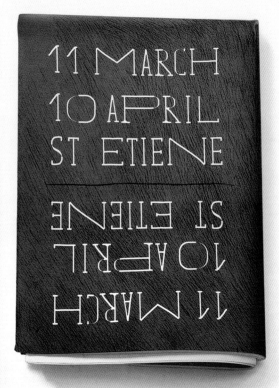
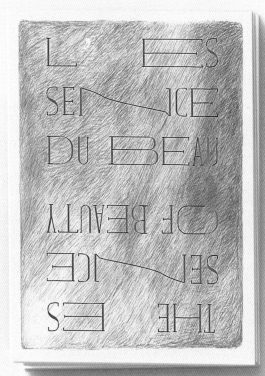

L'ESSENCE EST LA NATURE INTRINSÈQUE OU LA QUALITÉ INDISPENSABLE D'UNE CHOSE, QUI EN DÉFINIT SON CARACTÈRE.

Cette exposition réduit le large spectre des interprétations de la thématique générale « les sens du beau » vers une interrogation plus fondamentale en questionnant le design en tant que pratique à travers les travaux de la jeune et future génération de designers diplômés d'écoles Européennes de design. L'Essence du Beau montre les différentes capacités pour former une idée, de sa première expression sur le papier à sa concrétisation finale en produit prêt à satisfaire les besoins de consommateurs, en passant par la nécessaire confrontation aux recherches techniques et des matériaux inhérentes à la phase de prototypage.
Le design est ici exposé non seulement comme un résultat, mais également comme un procédé répondant çà unequestion, comme un moyen de transformer une idée en solution, réelle ou fictive, comme l'est la beauté.

THE ESSENCE IS THE INTRINSIC NATURE OR INDISPENSABLE QUALITY OF SOMETHING, WHICH DETERMINES ITS CHARACTER.

This exhibition reduces the wide range of interpretations of the general thematic "The Meanings of Beauty" to a more fundamental interrogation in questioning design as a practice through the works of the young and future generation of graduated designers from European schools of design.
The Essence of Beauty shows the different capacities to shape an idea, from its first expression on paper to its ending into a real product ready to satisfy consumers' needs, through the necessary confrontation with material and technical researches inherent to the prototyping phase.
Design is here exposed not only as a result, but also as a process answering to a question, as a way to transform an idea into a solution, whether real or fictitious, as beauty is.

63

TINO
SEUBERT

REVALVAINTE

YU
HIRAOTA

VE TIT Y

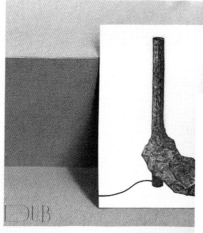

EDUB

FERREOL

BABIN

L'Essence du Beau

STUDIO AH-HA
with SAM BARON & CO

CLIENT
**Biennale Internationale
Design Saint-Étienne**

CITY
Paris, FR

These designs were created for L'Essence du Beau, an exhibition of talented young artists curated by Sam Baron for the Biennale Internationale Design Saint-Étienne. The font style and the materials used in the project represent the modern, avant-garde style that dominates during the Biennale events.

Molècula

JOSEP PUY

CLIENT
Personal project

CITY
Barcelona, SP

Promotional materials designed for Molècula, a festival that aims to share the techniques of molecular cuisine with the general public. The font and graphic elements, as well as the materials and techniques used, were selected to emphasize the fact that all five senses are an essential part of the gastronomic experience.

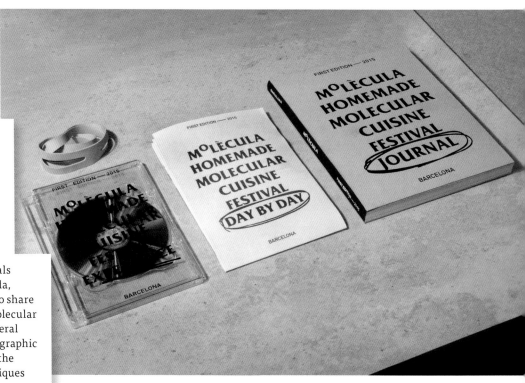

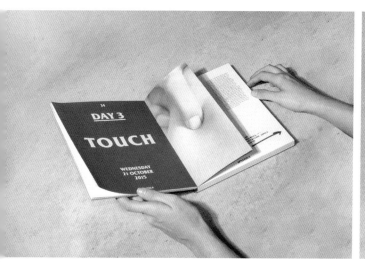

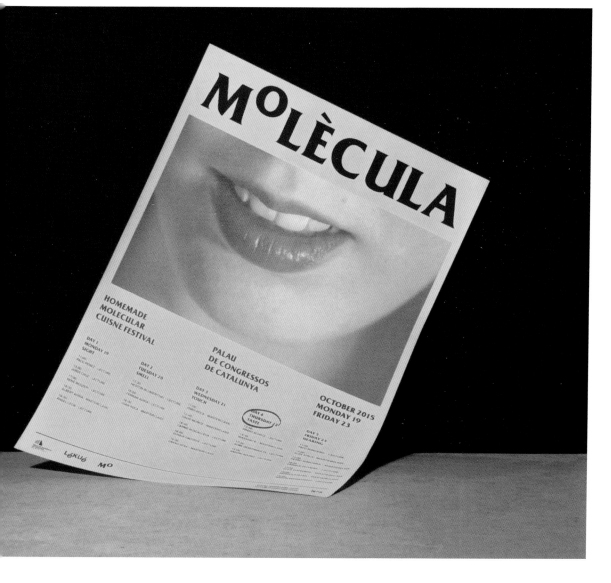

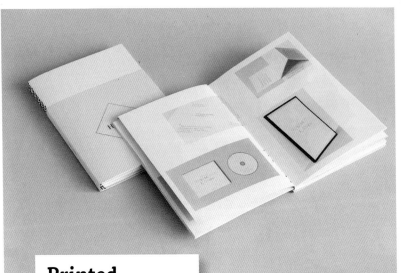

Printed Portfolio
LISA NEUREITER

CLIENT
Self-promotion

CITY
Graz, AT

Self-promotion portfolio presenting the designer's works in three different fields: personal projects, commissions for clients and personal information of interest. The sections are connected in the cover with a zig-zag. An interchangeable band at the centre of the first page allows for customization.

Personal Branding/ Print Portfolio
LISA NEUREITER

CLIENT
Self-promotion

CITY
Graz, AT

The power of the handwritten word in our digital times is emphasized in this portfolio of Lisa Neureiter's work. It includes a card that allows you to handwrite a message at the end of each project. The cover is made of wood, and the portfolio is hand bound.

Intership report
WENG NAM YAP

CLIENT
Self-promotion

CITY
Kuala Lumpur, MY

Promotional project documenting the designer's experiences in two design studios, based in Barcelona and in Prague. Both cities share the same colours in their flag, red and yellow. A centrefold map inside the book illustrates some of his experiences and travels during these periods.

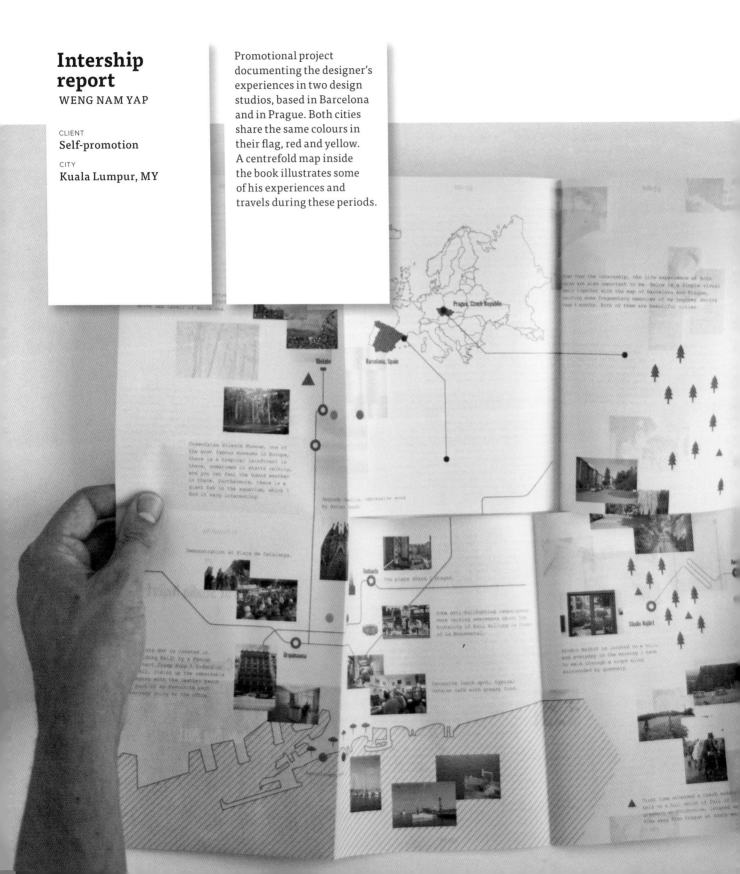

67

Irina Graewe Brochure
I LIKE BIRDS

CLIENT
**Irina Graewe-
Interiors Editor & Stylist**

CITY
Hamburg, DE

Stylist Irina Graewe asked I Like Birds to design the printed materials for the presentation of her portfolio. The project created by the studio included a lookbook, posters and postcards.

Summer Sunshine Expo
TSENG KUO-CHAN

CLIENT
Personal work

CITY
Taipei, TW

Designer Tseng Kuo-Chan produced the graphics for the photo exhibition Summer Sunshine. The poetic design of the invitations, leaflets and posters reproduces elements contained in the exhibited works.

Oitavos
Postcards

LOVE STREET STUDIO

DESIGNERS
**Joana Rangel,
Mª Carmo Mineiro**

CLIENT
The OItavos Hotel

CITY
Lisbon, PT

This series of postcards was created for the Oitavos hotel in Cascais (Portugal). It consists of a photographic tour that is also an emotional journey. Each postcard links an image of a place with a keyword that best defines it—for example, nature, light, history, sea or food.

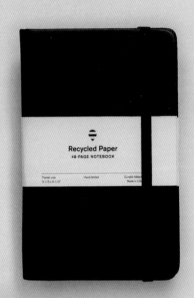

Recycled Paper
48-PAGE NOTEBOOK

⊜ Fundación Capital

⊜ Sucursal Colombia
Cra. 46 No. 102 — 42
Bogotá, Colombia

E info@fundacioncapital.org
T +57 (1) 602 5530

enviar a:

_____

_____

_____

Ayudando a familias de bajos recursos a mejorar y construir
un mejor futuro.

Fundación Capital.

E   info@fundacioncapital.org
T   +57 (1) 602 5530

Fundación
Capital
ANAGRAMA

CLIENT
Material Art Fair

CITY
**Monterrey,
Mexico City, MX**

Fundación Capital is a
nonprofit organization
with several bases in Latin
America. It focuses its
efforts on the fight against
poverty and exclusion.
Anagrama's logo design
was inspired by the bee,
an animal that symbolizes
hard work and organization.

Fundación Capital.

E info@fundacioncapital.org
T +57 (1) 602 5530

☌ Sucursal Panamá
Torre de las Américas, Torre B, Piso 15
PO Box : 0832 — 00155 WTC
Punta Pacífica, Panamá.

☌ Sucursal Colombia
Cra. 46 No. 102 — 42
Bogotá, Colombia.

Fecha:

Bienvenido a Fundación Capital,
cientos de la inclusión financiera e incubadora
de innovación en la creación de activos,
que trabaja para eliminar la pobreza.

fundacioncapital.org

Fundación
Capital $1.80

☌ Fundación Capital.

Fundación Capital está celebrando los
5 años que lleva trabajando para
erradicar la pobreza, estimular el ahorro
y promover la inclusión.

fundacioncapital.org

Fundación Capital.

E info@fundacioncapital.org
T +57 (1) 602 5530

☌ Sucursal Panamá
Torre de las Américas, Torre B, Piso 15
PO Box : 0832 — 00155 WTC
Punta Pacífica, Panamá.

☌ Sucursal Colombia
Cra. 46 No. 102 — 42
Bogotá, Colombia.

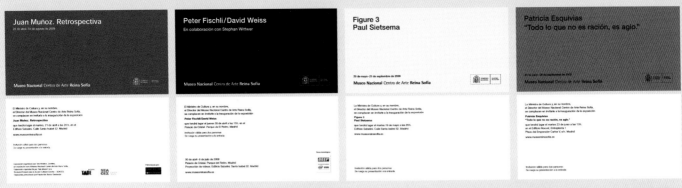

MNCARS postcards
EL VIVERO

CLIENT
**Museo Nacional Centro
de Arte Reina Sofia**

CITY
Madrid, SP

Madrid-based design team El Vivero created a collection of postcards to advertise the exhibitions and events of the Museo Nacional Centro de Arte Reina Sofía. The project centres on simple and powerful typography and a single image.

Juan Muñoz. Retrospectiva
22 de abril - 31 de agosto de 2009

Julio González
11 de marzo - 1 de...

ARCO 2009

Eulalia...

Peter Fischli / David...

David Maljkovic

feliz 2009

Frances...
14 de octubre de 200...

Ro...
De...
20 de...

24 de junio - 28 de septiembre de 2009
Museo Nacional Centro de Arte Reina Sofía

MUSEO NACIONAL
CENTRO DE ARTE
REINA SOFÍA

zelfbestuursstraat 12-14 rue de l'autonomie, 1070 brussels - belgium
tel +32 2 522 08 40, fax +32 2 523 45 00 www.monodot.be

zelfbestuursstraat 12-14
12-14 rue de l'autonomie
1070 brussels - belgium
tel +32 2 522 08 40
fax +32 2 523 45 00
www.monodot.be

zelfbestuursstraat 12-14 rue

zelfbestuursstraat 12-14 rue de l'autonomie, 1070 brussels - belgium
tel +32 2 522 08 40, fax +32 2 523 45 00
www.monodot.be

zelfbestuursstraat 12-14
12-14 rue de l'autonomie
1070 brussels - belgium
tel +32 2 522 08 40
fax +32 2 523 45 00
www.monodot.be

zelfbestuursstraat 12-14 rue

zelfbestuursstraat 12-14 rue de l'autonomie, 1070 brussels - belgium
tel +32 2 522 08 40, fax +32 2 523 45 00 www.monodot.be

zelfbestuursstraat 12-14 rue de l'autonomie, 1070 brussels - belgium
tel +32 2 522 08 40, fax +32 2 523 45 00 www.monodot.be

zelfbestuursstraat 12-14
tel +32 2 522 08 40, fax +32 2
www.monodot.be

maarten le roy
executive producer
+32 496 53 83 73
maarten@monodot.be

73

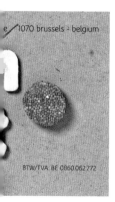

Monodot

ME STUDIO

CLIENT
Monodot

CITY
Amsterdam, NL

The starting point for this playful project created by Monodot, a film production company based in Brussels, involved asking the firm's partners to fill a shoebox with their favourite small round objects (such as buttons, sweets, coins and jewellery). These little items were used to form the letter "O," which appears three times in the company's name. Different combinations of letters and objects form a wide variety of business cards.

Nuzyn now at suikerdepôt

Nuzyn is a travelling store which sells timeless fashion and basics for men and women. Each item is carefully chosen and tells the story of the designer. The collections contain a mix of handmade, hand-dyed and 100% organic pieces.

collection:
Geoffrey B. Small, Jeroen van Tuyl, HrVi, Mykita & Karel Faber

Tee's and jeans
a project by Jos van Heel, Netty Nauta and Annet Schukkink

a collection of customized t-shirts and 501 jeans, photography by Marc de Groot, Astrid Zuidema & Kira Buns

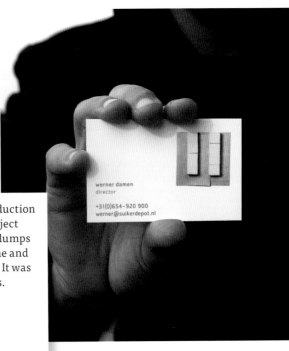

Suikerdepôt
ME STUDIO

CLIENT
Suikerdepôt

CITY
Amsterdam, NL

Suikerdepôt is an independent film production company based in Amsterdam. This project plays on the firm's name by using sugar lumps as the central element in a stationery line and complementary promotional materials. It was shortlisted for the Dutch Design Awards.

suikerdepot.com

ENJOY

suikerdepôt
prinsengracht 463 bg, 1015 hp amsterdam, the netherlands
info@suikerdepot.nl, +31(0)20-775 20 77
www.suikerdepot.nl

EXPO

opening at suikerdepôt
november the 5th, from 6 till 9pm

collection for sale untill december the 4th
thursdays to fridays from 11 till 5pm

prinsengracht 463 bg, 1016hp - amsterdam
www.suikerdepot.nl / +31 (0)20 7752077

with thanks to: House of Orange, Irena Ruben,
Marie Louise Toetenel and Zipper (Amsterdam)

SD

info@suikerdepot.nl

Karolina Mika
VIVID STUDIO

CLIENT
Karolina Mika

CITY
Kracó**w, PL**

Cracovian Vivid Studio created the branding identity for fashion designer Karolina Mika. The project revolves around three black-and-white illustrations that are repeated throughout the business cards, packaging, bags and labels that the project comprises. The result is a strong logo created with the first letters of the client's name and a linear, monochrome and dynamic collection that reflects the spirit of the brand.

karolina mika
790 36 13 00

WWW.KAROLINAMIKA.PL

Beck
STUDIO AH—HA

CLIENT
Beck Seat Covers

CITY
Lisboa, PT

The timeless, simple pleasure of riding along on two wheels provided the inspiration for this branding and packaging project for Beck, an innovative firm that designs seat covers for scooters.

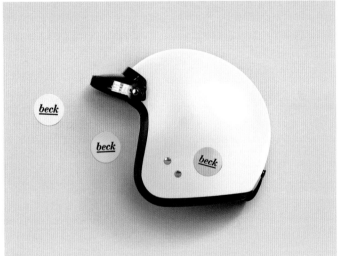

Develops
TRAPPED IN SUBURBIA

DESIGNERS
**Karin Langeveld,
Cuby Gerards,
Richard Fussey**

CLIENT
Develops

CITY
The Hague, NL

Sandra van Vliet of Develops was inspired by the sketches that she produces to explain her ideas to her clients. She converted some of them into designs for letterheads, business cards, notepads and envelopes. The simple aesthetic emphasizes agile communication and exchanges of ideas.

Requena

ANDRÉS REQUENA

CLIENT
Self-promotion

CITY
Barcelona, SP

These cards were part of Andrés Requena's promotional campaign for his graphic design business.

Recreo
True Stories
ANDRÉS REQUENA

CLIENT
Recreo.eu

CITY
Barcelona, SP

This periodically updated series of humorous illustrations is shared through Instagram by Andrés Requena. The conceptual illustrations include puns, social criticism and his personal take on the world. Andrés's most successful pieces have been printed in postcard format.

79

Connecting the Dots

JI-YOUNG JEON

CLIENT
Self-promotion

CITY
Seoul, KR

The station points in this promotional project based on a metro map represent milestones in designer Ji-Young Jeon's career. Each line that passes through the points has a special meaning: the red D Line shows his work as a graphic designer, H Line his accomplishments as an art student, and C Line his achievements from both areas.

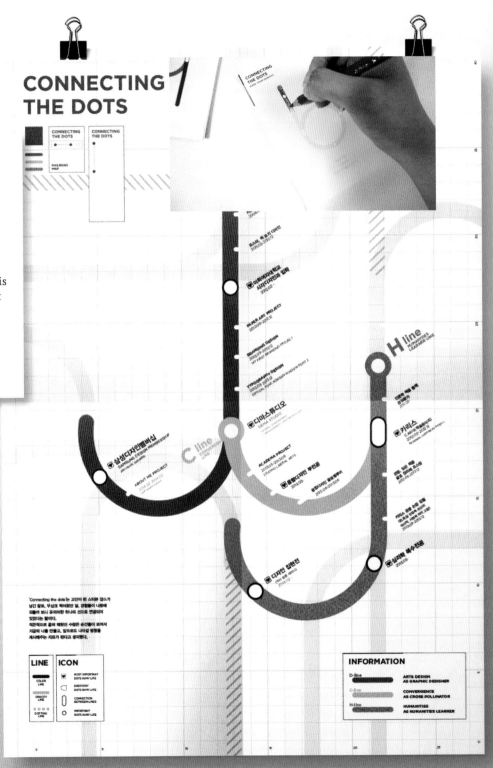

CONNECTING THE DOTS
MAKE YOUR IDENTITY

you
can
know

who
you
are

Greetings from
Kivalina, Alaska

Greetings from
The Pechora Sea, Russia

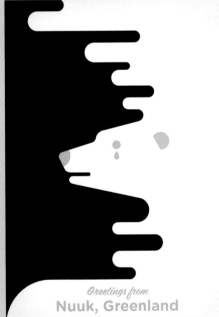

Greetings from
Nuuk, Greenland

Greetings from
Kirkenes, Norway

Arctic Postcards
HUMAN AFTER ALL

DESIGNERS
**Paul Willloughby,
Angus MacPherson,
Eve Lloyd Knight**

CLIENT
Weapons of Reason

CITY
London, UK

Weapons of Reason is a publication focused on exposing the global issues that affect our world. Illustrators Anna Lloyd Knight and Eva Dunn produced these four original postcards to raise awareness of the effects of climate change in the Arctic.

A Guide to
Making Things
HEY

CLIENT
Fieldwork

CITY
Barcelona, SP

To celebrate their first anniversary, Manchester-based company Fieldwork decided to send a gift to their clients and team members. Hey Studio designed eight postcards illustrating ideas that reflect the company's work and identity, to create a perfect Guide to Making Things.

Taidehalli
TSTO

DESIGNERS
**Matti Kunttu,
Antti Uotila**

CLIENT
Taidehalli

CITY
Helsinki , FI

The Taidehalli is one of the most important contemporary art centres in Finland. The design agency Tsto was given the task of designing its new branding. Tsto took inspiration from the architecture of the building, which was designed by Jarl and Hilding Ekelund and built in 1928. The logo appears on the art centre's postcards and other promotional materials.

EXPRESSIONIST UND VISIONÄR
DES WOHNENS
–

WENZEL HABLIK

04. AUG. – 29. SEPT. 2013

GALERIE IM MARSTALL AHRENSBURG

Ergänzender Ausstellungsteil im
Schloss Ahrensburg

Öffnungszeiten:
Galerie: Fr, Sa, So 11 bis 17 Uhr
Schloss: Sa und So 11 bis 17 Uhr

www.galerie-im-marstall.de

Ahrensburg Gallery
I LIKE BIRDS

CLIENT
Galerie Ahrensburg
CITY
Hamburg, DE

I Like Birds was hired by
the Ahrensburg Gallery
to produce the printed
materials for the art
exhibition *Expressionist und
Visionär des Wohnens—
Wenzel Hablik*. The project
includes invitations, flyers,
posters and banners, as well
as a large floor decal for the
Hamburg Central Station.

»DIE WIRKLICHKEITEN
VON HEUTE SIND
DIE UTOPIEN
VON GESTERN.«

WENZEL HABLIK

85

Vuoden Huiput

TSTO

DESIGNERS
**Inka Järvinen,
Matti Kunttu,
Antti Uotila**

CLIENT
**Grafia – Association
of Visual Communication
Designers in Finland**

CITY
Brooklyn, NY, USA

Since 1980, the visual identity of Vuoden Huiput, an annual advertising and design competition held in Finland, has been based on a pyramid shape. For the 2013 event, Tsto created a continuing visual identity that changed throughout the year. It relies on the shape of the pyramid and plays with the idea of searching for the pyramid in the deepest jungles & murkiest undiscovered lands.

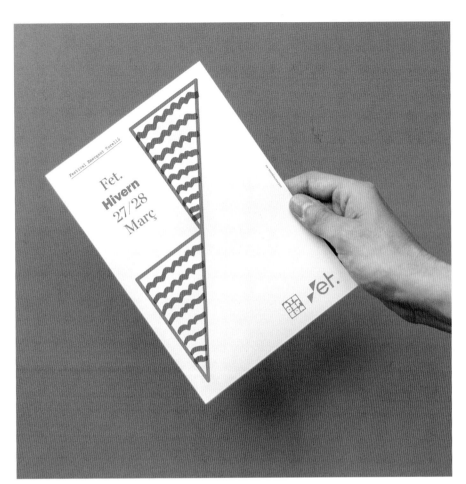

Fet Hivern
ANDRÉS REQUENA

CLIENT
Fet

CITY
Barcelona, SP

Andrés Requena designed these branding materials for the Festival Emergent de Torelló, which takes place in northeastern Spain. The central element is a flight of stairs, which is used as a metaphor for the word "emergent."

ArtFad 2014
HEY

CLIENT
ArtFad

CITY
Barcelona, SP

The idea behind these promotional cards for ArtFad: Arts and Contemporary Craft Awards was to draw the profile of a geometric "A" and then customize it with different patterns and materials. The invitations were made using Maxon comic patterns. The only machine-based process was the printing of the text and lines. The designers bought one hundred copies, which were later customised one by one, resulting in five hundred unique invitations.

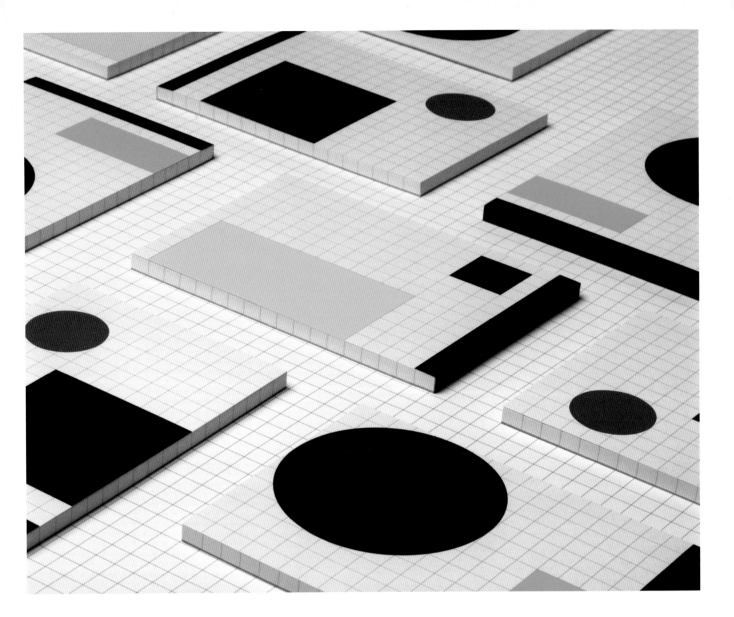

Notebooks
HEY

CLIENT
Self-promotion

CITY
Barcelona, SP

These graph paper notebooks were designed by Hey Studio to take notes, capture ideas, sketch or simply leave a special message of thanks.

Design
Museum

BOND

DESIGNERS
**Jesper Bange,
Christofer Goertz,
Annika Peltoniemi**

ESTRATEGY
Arttu Salovaara

PRODUCER
Marina Kelahaara

CLIENT
Design Museum

CITY
Helsinki, FI

The Helsinki Design Museum chose Bond as its partner for a development project aimed at increasing the visibility of the museum and improving its visitor experience. Inspired by the golden age of Finnish design, the visual identity of the museum was reworked and subsequently used on cards, promotional flyers, posters and the museum's website.

Self-Promo Mailer

BRIAN BILES

CLIENT
Academic work

CITY
Laguna Beach, CA, USA

Printed on both sides,
this fold-out brochure
designed by Brian Biles
is part of his promotional
material, which includes
a personalized logotype
and printed portfolio.

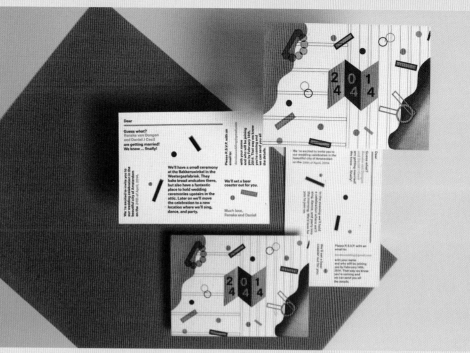

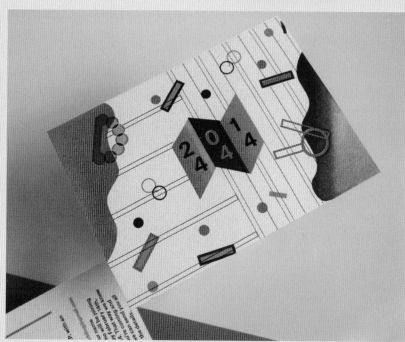

D&R
MARTA VELUDO

CLIENT
D&R

CITY
Amsterdam, NL

This project consists of the graphic design and illustration for a wedding invitation commissioned by a young couple named Daniel and Remske: risograph printing using two colours and a fluorescent dye.

Piet Mondrian's Exhibition Invitation

JOANNA ZOFIA
KRZEMPEK

CLIENT
Academic project

CITY
Gdansk, PL

For the opening of
a Mondrian retrospective,
an alluring invitation
was designed conveying
the character of his work.
The result plays to
perfection with geometry,
creating a network of
colours which is quickly
associated with the
Dutch artist's paintings.

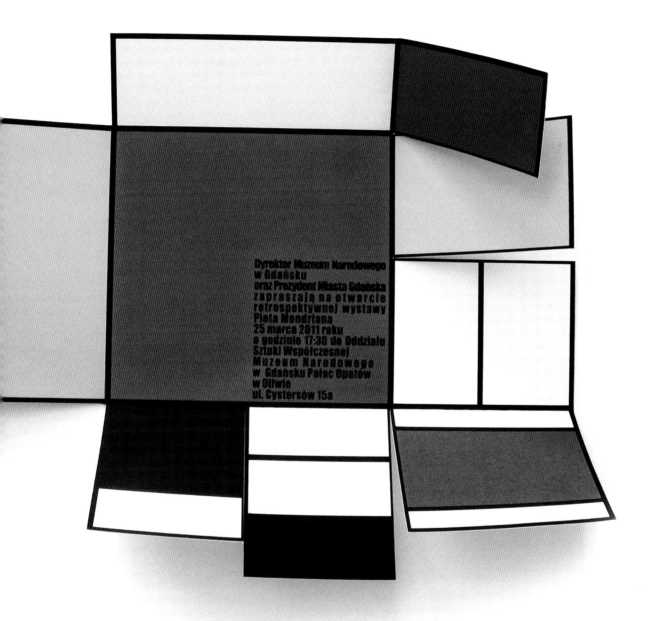

Dyrektor Muzeum Narodowego
w Gdańsku
oraz Prezydent Miasta Gdańska
zapraszają na otwarcie
retrospektywnej wystawy
Pieta Mondriana
25 marca 2011 roku
o godzinie 17:30 do Oddziału
Sztuki Współczesnej
Muzeum Narodowego
w Gdańsku Pałac Opatów
w Oliwie
ul. Cystersów 15a

OUR BRAND GUIDELINES

THE McGUIRE PROGRAMME
BEYOND STUTTERING

STRONGER TOGETHER

One programme, one unified presence.

The McGuire Programme is constantly growing, expanding into new territories and helping more people overcome their stutters than ever before.

As we grow, it is essential that we take great care of our brand. We need to all look, feel and speak as one united programme. Doing this will reinforce the trust and good reputation we have with our audience and peers, and help us to stand out from our competitors.

When creating any communications, please refer to this document to ensure that it is appropriate and effective. These guidelines are a useful set of simple rules and guides that explain how our brand works most effectively. Examples and template designs have been created which may be given to local designers, printers, or press publications, ensuring that the McGuire Programme speaks clearly and effectively, wherever it is in the world.

A WORLD WHERE PEOPLE WHO STUTTER CAN SPEAK FREELY

AND BE THE PERSON THEY WANT TO BE

The McGuire Programme g
beyond overcoming your st
it transforms people who st
into articulate, well spoken

We don't just concentrate o
speech, but the person as a

MMM

Our typeface
Garage Gothic

BE BOLD

REGULAR
BOLD
BLACK

What is Garage Gothic?
Garage Gothic is a bold and distinctive typeface. It strikes the fine balance of being authoritative and rugged, with friendly and approachable.

There are three weights of Garage Gothic at our disposal.

When do I use Garage Gothic?
Used to create impact, Garage Gothic is perfect for headlines and call to actions. Avoid using Garage Gothic for large amounts of text, such as body copy. Avoid using Garage Gothic at text sizes smaller than 9pt.

Our most frequently used weight is Garage Gothic Bold, for situations such as headlines, but we do use Regular for situations such as the Keyprint descriptor on our logo.

How do I use Garage Gothic?
To ensure consistency when setting text using Garage Gothic please adhere to the following guidelines outlined on this page. All these adjustments can be made either in your InDesign Toolbar or the 'Paragraph Style Options' palette. For maximum impact we always set Garage Gothic in upper case.

Note:
We do not use Garage Gothic in large amounts of body text, use it for impactful headlines only.

Kerning and tracking
The kerning for Garage Gothic Bold should be set to 'Optical' and tracking set to (-35) (see right).

Leading
The leading should always be 20% smaller than the type size (see right).

When using very large headlines the leading can be adjusted visually.

Hyphenation
Automatic hyphenation should be switched off for your layout.

Justification
Word Spacing should be set to Minimum 80%, Desired 80% and Maximum 80% (see right).

Case
We always use Garage Gothic in upper case.

Our positive impact

POSITIVE IMPACT

Our blue speech bubble plays the role of highlighting the positive impact that the McGuire Programme can have for people.

Why the speech bubble?
Taken from our logo, the speech bubble is a flexible device which helps us communicate the positive impact of the McGuire Programme.

Used in text
As illustrated in this document, the speech bubble may be used in text, drawing our attention to key messages.

Used in illustration
The speech bubble may also be used in illustration, again highlighting the positive impact of the McGuire Programme.

Where can I get the speech bubble?
The speech bubble is available to download from the 'McGuire Programme Brand Assets' folder on Dropbox.

Our tone of voice is direct, impactful and succinct. We don't waffle, we formulate our message and deliver it with authority, with confidence and charm.

The role of the speech bubble
We use the speech bubble device to draw emphasis to a particular part of our message - whenever possible the message should reflect the positive impact of the McGuire Programme.

NEGATIVE POSITIVE

VICTIM ATHLETE

FEAR FUN

SPEAKING FROM EXPERIENCE

BEEN THERE DONE THAT CONQUERED IT

Why do we use illustration?
Illustration is a cost effective and flexible way of expressing unique and varied messages. We try to use intelligence and wit in all McGuire communications.

Illustration style
Our vector illustrations are bold, confident, and impactful. Our style is simple and iconic.

Type with text
We may also use our typefaces (Garage Gothic and Georgia) in creative ways to bring messages to life, such as 'Hello' / 'Hetter' and 'Deliberate Dysfluency' as shown here.

Can I use the illustrations in the document?
Absolutely! You can download all of the illustrations used in this document from the McGuire Programme Brand Assets' folder on Dropbox.

Can I create my own illustration in a specific message?
Please do! Just remember to follow the visual style outlined in this document to ensure consistency.

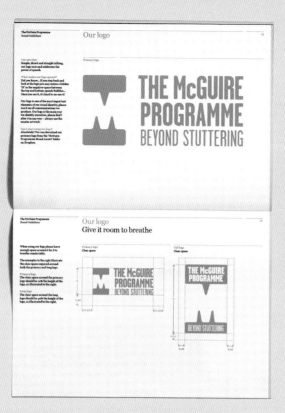

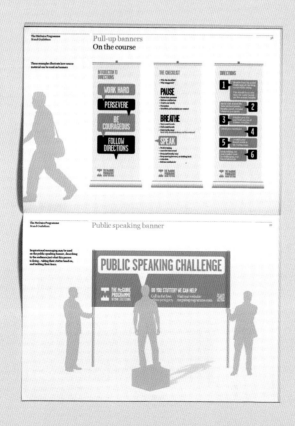

The McGuire Programme
PURPOSE

CREATIVE DIRECTOR
Stuart Youngs

PROJECT MANAGER
Rosie Buhler

DESIGNER
Sean Rees

CLIENT
The McGuire Programme

CITY
London, UK

Design of brand identity for The McGuire Programme, an initiative providing therapeutic coaching to help those who stutter become articulate, eloquent speakers. Focusing on the core thought Beyond Stuttering, the new logo which presents an 'M' within the surrounding speech bubbles' negative space, serves to highlight the ways in which McGuire supports their patients. Bold graphic speech bubbles show the positive impact of the programme and witty illustrations are used to demonstrate how The McGuire Programme is transforming people's lives.

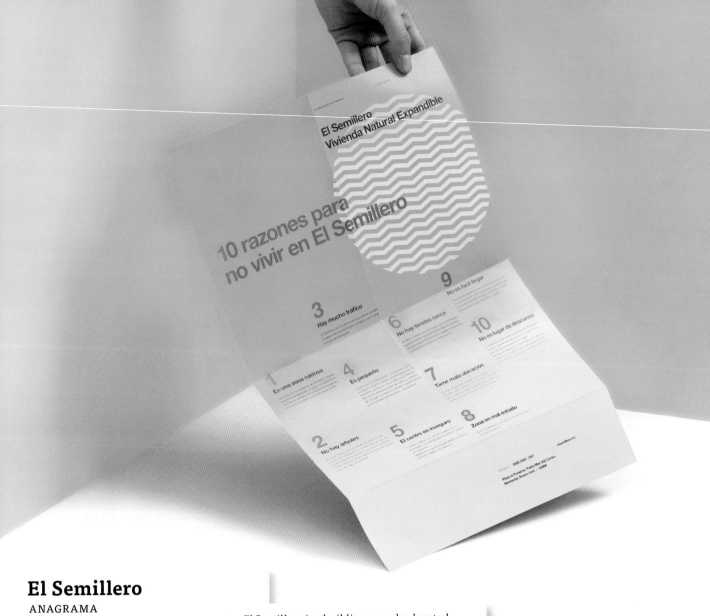

El Semillero

ANAGRAMA

CLIENT
Material Art Fair

CITY
Monterrey, MX

El Semillero is a building complex located in the heart of Monterrey, Mexico. It provides sustainable and affordable housing for young people. This leaflet that outlines the advantages of living in El Semillero is designed to create a sense of nature and open spaces through its use of citrus colours and illustrations.

94

Nueva Purísima.

El Semillero.
Vivienda Natural Expandible
T. 8344 1100

www.elsemillero.mx

Plaza la Purísima. Pedro Méx 401.
Monterrey, NL — 64000.

Fraterna,
experiencia inmobiliaria

Pladis, concepto arquitectonico

Espacios para todos

depa
modelo A

2R + 2B

depa
modelo B

2R + 1EF + 2B

depa
modelo C

2R + 2B

depa
modelo D

2R + 1 1/2B

15 ame-
nidades

Amplia tu comunidad
sustentable

95

Blaustein/Melting
MELINA PECHARKI

CLIENT
Kauf Dich Glücklich

CITY
Berlin, DE

This series of postcards was designed by Melina Pecharki for the Berlin-based fashion firm Kauf Dich Glücklich. The cards reproduce textures and colours of fabrics that the firm used in its collections between 2014 and 2015.

96

The Joy of Graphic Design
I LIKE BIRDS

CLIENT
Here We Go

CITY
Hamburg, DE

I Like Birds developed the branding, printed promotional materials and website for the Joy of Graphic Design festival, which takes place in Hamburg and promotes contemporary graphic design in the city.

Festival in Hamburg

28 – 30/09/12

Mario Lombardo
Erik Kessels
Andreas Uebele
Happypets
Robert Klanten
Vier5

rten Programm
ter:

ign.com

1st international Graphic Festival in Hamburg

28 – 30/09/12

Bureau Mirko
I Like Birds
Hello Me + Tim
Shake Your Tr
Deutsche & Ja
Mr. Pataki

»The Joy of Graphic Design« ist ein drei-
tägiges Grafikdesign Festival am Ober-
hafen in Hamburg mit internationalem
Symposium, Night-Workshops, Ausstel-

lung,
»ABO
Print
und I

Values

STUDIO CARRERAS

CLIENT
Personal work

CITY
London, UK

This project is a visual representation of the ideas that inspire us every day. It consists of fifty-eight cards that depict the human principles and values that motivate us to be who we are.

11 ♥
Spirituality emphasis on spiritual not material matters

42 ▲
Successful achieving goals

01 ♥
Broadminded tolerant of different ideas and beliefs

02 ♥
Equality equal opportunity for all

30 ■
Family Security safety for loved ones

12 ♥
Helpfulness working for the welfare of others

14 ♥
Forgiveness willing to pardon others

25 ■
Self Discipline self restraint, resistance to temptation

40 ▲
Social Power control over others, dominance

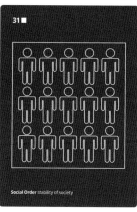

31 ■
Social Order stability of society

36 ▲
Social recognition respect, approval by others

39 ▲
Wealth material possessions, money

52 ●
Curious interested in everything, exploring

41 ▲
Influential having an impact on people and events

13 ♥
True Friendship close, supportive friends

49 ●
Daring seeking adventure, risk

Material Art Fair

ANAGRAMA

CLIENT
Material Art Fair

CITY
Monterrey, MX

When it was hired to produce branding and promotional materials for Material Art, a fair held in Mexico City that focuses on emerging artists, Anagrama produced designs that conveyed the essence of the event's personality, vitality and symbolism.

MATERIAL ART FAIR

DANIELA ELBAHARA
directora / director
daniela@material-fair.com +52 (55) 5256 5533
Mexico City

twitter@materialfair
facebook/material.fair

MATERIAL
CITY
MEXICO

MATERIAL
CITY
MEXICO

Contact Information
Mail / info@material-fair.com
www.material-fair.com

twitter profile / @materialfair
facebook page / materialfair
1 / (+53) 55-5256-5533

Calle Melchor Ocampo 154-A
Col. San Rafael, Del. Cuauhtémoc
C.P. 06470 Mexico City

MATERIAL ART FAIR

Contact Info /
info@material-fair.com
material-fair.com

DANIELA ELBAHARA
directora / director
daniela@material-fair.com +52 (55) 5256 5533
Mexico City

material-fair.com

twitter@materialfair
facebook/material.fair

MATERIAL
CITY
MEXICO

Contact Info /
info@material-fair.com
material-fair.com

Calle Melchor Ocampo 154-A
Col. San Rafael, Del. Cuauhtémoc
C.P. 06470 Mexico City

twitter profile / @materialfair
facebook page / materialfair
1 / (+53) 55-5256-5533

MATERIAL
CITY
MEXICO

Calle Melchor Ocampo 154-A
Col. San Rafael, Del. Cuauhtémoc
C.P. 06470 Mexico City

twitter profile / @materialfair
facebook page / materialfair
1 / (+53) 55-5256-5533

It's a Wrap!

MARTA VELUDO

COLLABORATORS
**Sue Doeksen,
Ricardo Leite**

CLIENT
**The Bookstore
Foundation**

CITY
Amsterdam,NL

This project comprises Christmas invitations that double up as wrapping paper. The A3 sheets risoprinted in 2 colours with a mash up of 10 different patterns, give to the invitation the playful wrap option. The result was an edition of 150 units, all one of a kind, sent in a wrapped tube.

Vingt-quatre
heures d'architecture
LES PRODUITS DE L'ÉPICERIE

CLIENT
Vingt-Quatre Heures d'Architecture

CITY
Paris, FR

A modular logo was used for the business cards, flyers, posters, stationery and other promotional materials for the architectural event Vingt-quatre heures d'architecture.

100

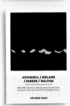

BBC Concert Orchestra postcards
STUDIO OUTPUT

DESIGN DIRECTOR
Dan Moore

DESIGNER
Lucy Gibson

CLIENT
BBC Symphony Orchestra

CITY
London, UK

Taking soundwaves as a graphic cue, Studio Output designed a campaign to promote a series of events at London's Southbank Centre. Forming part of The Rest is Noise season, the concerts set out to capture the spirit of the 20th century – and how music reflected its discords, wars and revolutions. Each one of the A6 postcards features a graphic, representing a tiny soundwave segment from a piece of music to be performed. By varying the colour palettes and carefully selecting waveforms, the images evoke the subject matter of the music.

**ADDINSELL / IRELAND
/ PARKER / WALTON**
*World War Two music and verse to stir the soul
writing music to lift the British populace during WWII*

THE HOME FRONT

SYMPHONY 'MATHIS DER MALER'
PAUL HINDEMITH
*The prequel to Hindemith's opera Mathis der Maler (Mathis the Painter)
Looks a lance at the banality of artistic oppression in Nazi Germany*

SEVEN DEADLY SINS

HARLEM (A TONE PARALLEL TO HARLEM)
DUKE ELLINGTON
*A leisurely walk through the New York district's
Sunday morning finery to the Cakewalk transformed post-war
era of the beginning Civil Rights movement*

HIDDEN VOICES

A STRANGER HERE MYSELF
KURT WEILL ARR. KIM H. KOWALKE
*A selection of iconic theatre songs including
What Good Would the Moon Be?, and My Ship*

KURT WEILL BERLIN TO BROADWAY

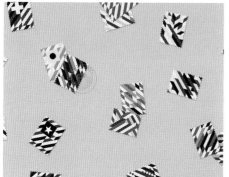

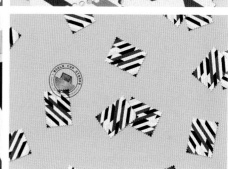

World Cup Stamps 2014

MAAN DESIGN STUDIO

DESIGNER
**Vitor Claro,
Pedro Lima Ferreira**

CLIENT
Personal project

CITY
Vila do Conde, PT

To celebrate the 2014 World Cup, MAAN Design Studio produced this unique collection of stamps that offer an original geometric twist on the flags of each competing nation.

FEB 12-13 LIMA

LATIN AMERICAN DESIGN FESTIVAL 2015

FEST.ORG

A8

A5

Latin American Design Festival 2015

IS CREATIVE STUDIO

DESIGNER
Richars Meza

CLIENT
Latin American Design

CITY
Lima, PE

The poster design and brand identity for the 2015 LAD Festival were inspired by the International Organization for Standardization's A series of paper sizes. Latin American identity is expressed through the use of neon colours that allude to the traditional fabrics of the Andean communities.

Perspectivism.

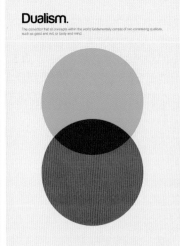

Dualism.

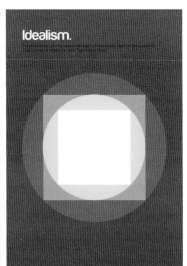

Idealism.

Determinism.

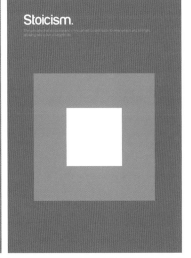

Stoicism.

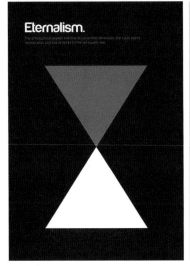

Eternalism.

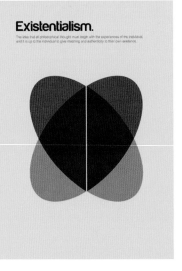

Existentialism.

Philographics
STUDIO CARRERAS

CLIENT
BIS Publishers

CITY
London, UK

Philographics is a series of ninety-five designs that explain philosophical concepts graphically through colours and simple shapes. The postcard-format designs are presented in a box and were published by BIS Publishers in 2014 in a book that features all the designs.

Capitalism.

Historicism.

Individualism.

Absolutism.

Syncretism.

Free will.

Philographics.
Genis Carreras

95 postcards
explaining big ideas
in simple shapes

AUTHORS INDEX

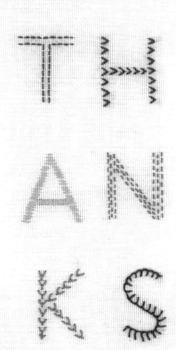